"There is no agony like bearing an untold story inside of you."
Zora Neele Hurston (b. 1891)

Zora 42

Musings-
Miss Keshia Shantae

Copyright © 2016 by Keshia Shantae

All rights reserved. This book or any portion thereof may not be reproduced or used in any manner whatsoever without the express written permission of the publisher except for the use of brief quotations in a book review.

Printed in the United States of America
First Printing, 2016
ISBN 978-0692615379

Indigo Lotus Publishing
90 Uvalde
Houston, TX 77015

Dedicated to My'Nyah Kryyst-al.
Always.
With homage to my Matriarch,
B.A.M.!

"HAIL MAMMA OF 10,000 NAMES!"

ZORA, GIOVANNI, SANCHEZ, SHANGE,
SESHAT, MOORE, RUCKER, BROWNE, SHEBA,
WALKER, SIMONE, JAMES, MORRISON,
JEZEBEL, BADU, HILL, SCOTT, HOOKS, BROOKS
DE VITA, OCTAVIA, JUNE, YEYE, ANGELOU,
LUCILLE, GWENDOLYN, AUDRE, ANGELINA,
PHILLIS, MERI, CISNEROS, JACKSON,
SOULJAH, BENSON, DUKES, KETURAH, SUNNI,
TUERE, CHAKA, AI, GRIMKE, RUBY,
WARSAN, CHRISTA, SASSAFRAS, RENEE,
NAYYIRAH, AJA, EARTHA, NABII,
TRETHEWAY, AND SO MANY, MANY MORE...

>Ether, 2007-2017

i. Tell My Horse
>Aire (Heir)   p. 13

II. Yeye
>Water   p. 37

III. Pixie
>Fyre   p. 69

IV. #poinsettasandbabymamas (2014)
>aEarth   p. 95

"TELL MY HORSE" Air {Aire, Heir}

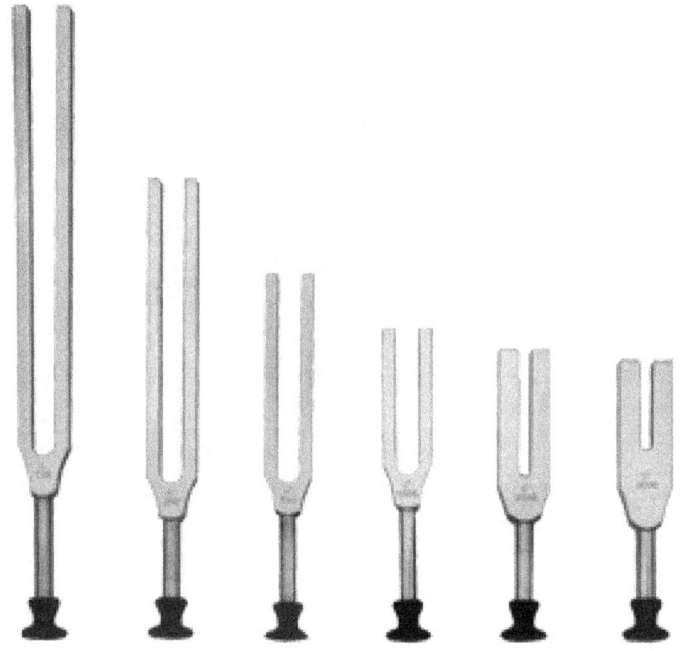

Unresolved

I wanted to run with Paul, we were under the Magnolia tree,

I wanted to run with Paul, we were under the Magnolia tree,

I wanted to run with Paul, we were under the Magnolia tree,

I had to leave Paul, now it's just Baby and me.

Ostara (also known as, 'Love is the Highest Form of Understanding')

sweet rain, quiet of dawn

lightening bolts, thunder growls in reply

strong winds, touch and tickle and bend

thick humidity, wett heat

She is thirsty.

to sprout and spread and grow and reach

to eat the Sun.

<u>Closer</u>
remember.
re-member...
...hold each other
closer.
tighter.
stronger.
let no space breathe between your bodies
may your souls meld together like steel
your minds sync into telepathy...
so when they try... them... they...
those who will suck the life out bone marrow
when they come for you
to separate you too-
even when s/he tries to push away
to walk away,
even when they run away...
there is no escape because you share the same breath.

cause this is the aftermath...
we are in the fallout

and the rules no longer apply......
never applied really...
and he is a target...
on the street corner and in the boardroom...
(phase him out, they say)
and she is a target...
her morals and decency and ability to nurture...
(phase her out, they say)
and we hurt the ones we love
and we hurt the ones who love us
and we are hurting
and no-one cares enough to offer a safe place...
just blame and denial and fear and blinders
and shame and fear and distractions and fear,
and fear and fear of death...
fear of living...
fear not.
heaven is inside.

heaven is between you and them, when
there is no confusion
when your embrace is so close you can see

inside their power
you can feel their power...
you can draw out their power...
you can recharge their power...
you become their power...
and they yours.
and nothing else matters...
and nothing else matters...
when nothing else matters...
then,

We are ready.

<u>La Luna</u>

I.   New Moon

Universal Blackness all around.

A sound.

Who's there?

In secrecy and omitted phrases

Under the cloak of darkness.

ii.   Under you.

Teeth, ears, nose-

I can't see you.

All the better to feel you.

Yes or No. "Here?" or "Here?"

We will have a look-

Once the sun is full and bright.

Visions of the day.

iii.   New moon.

Water engulfs and swells around you, visceral darkness.

What is this?

Warmth.

Sensation.

Thrill of salty potential,

Deep, nursing underground wells hidden from your eyes.

Dependable currents to carry us.

Darkness.

Angels

They're real.

For example, He and I

We make Angles.

That's when I see Angels.

And a lot of other bliss too.

That's what happens

When you form favorable angles

Sorta like

We was meant to cross paths.

Sorta like

With help from angels.

Yes, We must be.

We must be Stardust and sulfur and solve for his (x) and my (y) and where we meet is in the smiles of the angels.

Swing Low.
I arch my torso just so
at a perfect angle.

(I choose you.)

'We Real Cool'

"A little love goes a long way.. we have learned how to ration our affections, incase more does not come. We know how to create our own to tide us over. If love comes we rejoice. If it decides to pass us by, we do not cry. We have our reserves. Secret love in hidden places. We love ourselves enough to stay warm. We will not die from lack of love."

"We jazz June"

aint free, k.dot

subliminals be like:

"Girl its still game."

searching for meaning

dreaming

cant fuck an illusion

..aint me who 'spose to be choosin.

pimp c and bun b

on that pimp shit.

'niggy please'

my stilettos too high.....

aint free.

A poem, Miss U.S.A. (06/08/16)

Kali Maa,

So you telling me,

No.

If I keep identifying with "grassroot"

Under this new regime-

I will be plowed down (cee: Sandra).

Grassy roots iz outdated,

Too Earthen.

When this is an Air and Fire fight.

All green and hungry,

With no grocery stores.

Jes grass and roots and soo much water.

Atomic Dogg

These dogs

Underneath my window-

Going inn.

—-"That growl sounding real contrived girlie!"

Gotcha.

Againn.

3 Days Later, 4 Sandy. 7162015

"how terrorism works/she is me, easily/ i

already know what happened cause ive been there before. outspoken/ she showed those devils her fangs and they tore her apart/to prove a point/ just because/and for no reason other than, bow down black bitch/and i went a little crazy/and my sister had to heal me enuff, fill in the hole they keep diggin/her reiki

words/him/ his innerG when i needed it/ we need each other/cause this is how terrorism

works/this is the silent part of war/ the mind

fuck/ the chippin away at sanity, the weakening

of immune and emotion and spirit/ gunning for

our souls/ the soul-less ones/and every time i

see them, i look through them/a little

terrified cause my mouth is black like fuck

you/eloquently articulate, like "i know my

rights pig"/i have the right to remain silent/i have the right to remain violent/my rites/ my rites/ my rites/ love self, love family, love friends and a-alikes, love community, love the nation we build with each seed/ love in spirals, deep and all powerful black holes/black, no one escapes/ fuck terror/i know y, fear of a black universe.

Sub-Levels

you are a prophetic dream

an unpleasant nightmare

of water rising quickly and of tornadoes-

a hurricane of blood-thirsty vampires

with no guarantees of eternal life

just drowning and draining

predatory feasting

and chasms of charm

lifetimes

charms and spells for no reason other than

shoveling churchyard dirt into an empty coffin.

Grand Master Teacher Bobby Hemmitt
or titled, The Upside Room

This
Tree of life.
This arbor of knowledge,
Good and Evil
You was warned to avoid.

These
Empty shells
Walking around
Babbling loud and angry
Hell.
They say Angels whisper,
As if Hope is a secret.
The audacity
To dream and not follow through.
Looks like this:
Believing
In
God
But blind-eye avoiding

Evil,
In front-
You're behind.

Sometimes
I come
Here
Alone.
Not the empathetic 'alone',
The warrior's version.
The path of the chosen
And accepted.
The path I machete chopped myself

We fire-breathe and lotus-pose
Then hear voices

Inside.
Like schizophrenia -
No,
Im not off
Kilter.

Green and Brown
Earth.
pH balanced
She was made
with bounty
Yet them see division
Subtracted until Earth was
What it now is,
Unequal.
Out of equilibrium,
Yes.
No.
We are not the same.
Some add.
Some subtract.
This is how it iz.
Looking at The Tree
Listening to the roots.

Root works

Leaves and flowers
Branches and trunks of life
Here before us,
Ancient watcher.
Ginko and Elder and Magnolia,
Pineal Pinecones.
Carry a seed under my tongue,
Gather in Her groves-
Dancing naked under moonlight
"and everything like that."

Teacake

Rose: "...if I leave.. will he be able to find me.. will he come looking for me, or will he replace me with another Caroline... if I leave.. I must leave... the air, the water, the food, those sworn to lead and teach and protect... this place is past.. I must leave.. mind then body......will he come for me... will he follow after my tracks until he again smells my perfume.... will he hold my picture and ask each passer by if they know me.... will he pray to his ancestors for clues... if not... if he doesnt try.. wont try to find me.... if he shruggs his shoulders and doesnt ask where im going and if there's room for him too.... when he's ready to leave......he never was my Paul... my Paul would come for me... wouldnt let me leave without him...."

"The Black Freighter"

What if you worked for a racist?

what if you work for anyone outside your community collective, unbound by honor, love and justice?

what if u work cuz thats how u eat.. live..

nvrmnd smelly cheese and water wafers.

we simply pushing up the bottom rung. class distinctions. this workshop. where we work cause we're hungry. to prevent our babies from knowing hunger.

government dependency.

we're guarded and assaulted.

worker bees, not fly by niteflowers.

we know. (eyes veiled, mouths gagged, hands ties, feet nailed.)

And

Us

Wearing our Monkey Masks.

Until...

(Just You Wait.)

Sang it, High Priestess Nina.

II. YEYE (Wata)

Already Gone, Yeye Esesu.

I hesitated and debated

Reluctant to dive, headfirst into my own

Deep, dark uncharted waters...

Figured the shallow,

Moderately deep was safe.

Made me feel secure and comfortable,

Not like the feeling of feet off dry land

Wanted to stand on sand that didn't move

Didn't cover my feet and pull me under

Reluctantly resisted the pull of undercurrent...

Objected to giant squid and octopi,

Electric eels and stinging jellyfish

The unknown and unnamed life thriving in the

caves and vents way down where the sun doesnt

penetrate....

I ignored siren and mermaid songs

Calling me home..

Scared if i showed my scales, I would no longer belong

To you, them

On dry land.

No city-dwelling man could understand the trade-off..

Not he and she who arent called by the sea.

Therefore I contorted and convinced myself,

I couldn't breathe under water..

Kept my memory of waves and salt buried....

Funny how treasures hide from pirates

Then make themselves known to their owners...

Float to the surface after a terrible storm.

I didn't even need to search long.....

Maps guiding my feet home..

Olokun bending on coral knee

Marrying me.

Waning Moon Reversal Spell (1)

God

Is.

God is.

God

Is

Goddess.

God Is Goddess.

Spells.

God is Goddess.

God-Is.

God-iss.

God-ess.

Goddess.

God.

Godess.

God

Is.

Goddess.

is

God.

(Twirl 32xs and Repeat.)

Woman-ish

He needed motivation/ I needed stimulation/long hours we both grindin'/our reward/sex magick/ energy manipulation.

I put his hands on my pelvis/pushed up on his ego/ shake, shake, shake/ said, "When I move don't let go"/gimme what I come for/came for his lover's rock/rock steady/dig deeper for the key/and she'll overflow ya levee/whaaaa?

He needed a special juju/I told him, "Call me Yeye Susu."

_32.5_

and how to not look at the politics and banking systems of the brutes (Britain) and the EU as mine/aint mine/where my mines and my republics/their system is crashing/or is it?/you know those knights templar, labor legislators, servants of the crown lie/its sorta amazing tho/17.5 million people vs 15 million people/thats a whole heap of people..... then we got this whole clinton and trump/reality show

87% (also titled, Vulnerable)

"us/with our babies/tied to our backs/suckling at our breasts/exploring, not too far from our knees/ us/single mommies/sweating and struggling to keep it together/it, our family/without our men/to help/carry the babies, protect us from predators.. us/fill hungry little bellies/teach the is and ain't's/ us/we cling to each other/form alliances and support groups... girlfriends and friend-enemies/ us/we laugh and cry and cuss/talk shit about 'what that naga did' or 'didn't do'/us/we/...smile/ with pleasure/...longing/and wonder/when we see them/you/your family/your husband/your perfect universe/your husband/daddy who wants his family/lover man/its a beautiful thing/you and yours/and sometimes, it hurts a little... even though/i wouldn't trade/us."

Iron Deficient

Now,

Here.

Who bends iron?

Breaks and builds

  Our locks,

     Our Weapons,

         Our ceremonial masks?

Here,

No one.

No one.

Here.

  Not here.

No, Oggun is not here.

"Baby, Baby. Let's Go!! Now."

Here

We call Oggun.

We speak his name and ask him to come.

He does not answer.

He will not

Accept our offerings

Here.

He is not

Here.

Not here.

Can't be here.

Not mighty warrior Oggun.

Not here.

Jesus?

Yes.

Peace and turn the other cheek,

Forgiveness and long, long, long suffering.

Yes. Yes.

Jesus lives here,

Not Oggun.

Not

Here.

His time has passed.

Past.

It is too late.

It is much too late.

Must be,

Must have missed his powerful machete.

Must have missed his forest green and blueish-red lava.

Here,

Just cooled baptism waters

Now.

Here.

"Baby, Baby. Lets Go!!!! Now.

Now.

Now."

St. (High) John, The High Conqueror

(for Georgia Anne Muldrow)

Criss Cross, Apple Sauce

A five-pointed star

When you close your eyes to see

Does your vision take you far?

Into the dark

Into the deep

Into the oceans unknown

Are you scared?

Why do you fear?

When you came here naked and alone?

From where?

What happened first?

Before that spark of conception?
For what purpose?

To accomplish what?

Have you studied your lessons?

Spiral, Spiral

Around and around

Back where you started, you've returned.

Did you progress?

Did you move forward?

What advancement have you earned?

Sight, Smell, Hearing, Taste

Have you ever touched a rainbow?

7 bands playing 7 chords

Is that a tune you know?

Where does the music go?

Inside it goes

Down and up it goes

Through your organs and your pipes

Shaking, rattling, trembling, vibrating

Multiplying, increasing light.

2 dimensions, 3 dimensions

To think, it started from a simple dot-

That big bang, expanding spark.

Bang, Bang!

Boom!

Bump, Bump!

Thump!

Movements, actions, energies- Life.

Vibrations, the world is in constant formation

Push- Pull!

Death.

For everything,

Everything -

Has its price.

Hexed (Spinster)

'We' don't marry.

We Can't.

Not us.

Not us with secret names.

Wild flowers.

Wild,

Hexed.

(6)

I blame Her.

Mitochondrial DNA.

Her say, "Don't do it."

I blame The Real Housewives and Love and Hip-Hop too.

And Lady Brooks-DeVita, Ph.D's Women's Lit. course in undergrad:

"After marriage they drive you madd, lock you in your own upstairs attic, then siphon your Inheritance. Its in the literature, Jane Eyre for starts."

Hexed.

She a Bird, Pt. 2 (not really for Matti [FTB] b.u.t. inspired by "For Matti, Pt. 1. Written after her Mister called her a Bird.)

My Ancestors, Sing to me.

Red Bird, Red Bird.

These angry, wounded womb wenches. Hyenas. Low vibration, energy leeches.

On my prayer mat, petitioning for protection. Quieting, dissolving fear.

Arrived at my Justice and the front doors refused to unlock so we can make the company money- 'Her' received disciplinary actions consequently.

—―—―

News is, that other 'Brawd' drove her car into a ditch.

Good.

Red Bird, Red Bird.

"Thank You."

My Ancestors,

Sing to me.

"Sing Song Psalm Birds."

Derric Grey, B.More

I.

i rather be like, "he handlin' it."

#riots

II.

Yeye: "Rite Now.

Make More (B)abies! More scientists and soldiers.

A'more.

Babies.

Babies, Babies, Babies, Babies, Babies, Babies, Babies!!!!!!"

III.

#tooslow #rabbitholes #riddlemethis #rituals #alreadygone #thinkthinkthink #Work

IV. Decoded

They killed your beloved Belle Betsy Blue. Meanwhile Mars was directly above watching (hungry).

    "DEY POST_RACIAL LYNCHED THOSE BABIES!"

Planetary and Star alignments- "The Messiah is reborn everyday. Dem repeat, 'Don't let them have more babies.'"

...Not for nothing.

Southern Summers, Big Mama

"Sit'cho self down

And

Be still."

"shake team got it going on"

the whole world's gone madd

so imma keep shaking my ass

like bam, bam, bam

shaking up the cosmos

turning up the heat

hotter

humid even-

cause i said so

i control

my temperatures

this endurance feels like

keep dancing

even though

resistance hurts

and tomorrow

i won't move

until

the beat drops

and calls my body-

imma slave

to rhythm

my dna twists and turns

and dances

like the bodies

up

in the sky

where We

when We

dance to tones

like light.

Light around here keeps getting

darker

earlier

somebody changed the time

and then

everybody lost their minds

and desires

to dance

to come together....

to Capoeira....

to gather....

peacefully.

This world has gone madd

so imma keep shaking my ass

like bam, bam, bam...

like temple dancers skilled at

raising their vibration...

giving him something to fight for

there is a war

outside.

And his dances

his conditioning and training

his endurance

his Doundunba

is here.

Its in the downbeats,

while my booty tick is the upbeat.

Like tick tock.......
body rock.

Howling Wolf

'Magnetic like Magneto'

They think its just fiction.

Yo! They dead wrong tho.

<u>Saturn.</u>

its fear... fear of an uncontrollable force... i, as a woman, must volunteer to surrender, cuz the force comes naturally... its primal... and its winter in America... heaven help us all.

Jade Helm 15
(FB and Google are compromised. Over.)

There's A Riot Going On   0:00

III. Pixie (Fyre).

<u>al'Kah/i/na 20140705</u>

and the Women crafted Martial Fighting the Art in War.

Now,

Remember.

Get Low.

(Belly to tha flo')

DVD

He 1: D is for Dog.

He 2: No. D is for Daleth.

He 1: Whats that? Da-leth? D is for Dollars.

He 2: Daleth means Door. Its value is 4.

He 1: Where? In the alphabet? Nah, D is for Dead.

He 2: In Kaballah... Jewish Mysticism.... Sorcery.

He 1: Sorcery? Bro, thats the Devil.

He 2: Yes, thats D. D is Daath, begins with the Daleth symbol. Its numerical value is 4. The 4 worlds. Doors. "D".

He 1: K, that dope. I mean, D is for Dope. Rite?

He 2: Exact. D is Dimensions.

Anonymous.

In plain sight, they desecrate the temple... just as they burned down the trees and drowned the high priestess... and you don't remember... won't remember... remember what? you ask... ask.

"What is is?
I, is is...
Therefore, I must be...

Remember me?
When he was blinded, I helped him cee...
Worshipped him for 13 moons then,
Crafted his 14th peace.

Keep my name Sacred.
Remember me.
I, is is.
Therefore, I must be...

She. She be
Nephthys...

Neb-Het...
My ride or die.

They will...
It was written.
Remember me and I will...
Re- Member you."

Alkhemy

pots on the stove
simmer, boil and steam
tastes like "suga, dont forget"
tastes like "lust and love"
tastes like "no silverware needed"

pots on the stove
passion and sweat
preparation and patience
standing in this hott-ass kitchen
a cold sip of fresh lemonade

pots on the stove
worth every bite
my life.

<u>Zodiac</u>
winter ice storms
and
capricorn mountain goats make me forget
orange harvest skies.
feeling the season change
and my change
and no change
we need more change
and niggaz don't change
well,
sometimez they do.

all the time
it don't matter the season
or the symbol.
niggaz (be)
surrounding me
jade-eye asking, "where you think you goin'?"

sometimez,

my love.
i be
like
('B'-Lack..)
"dead them niggaz and that nigga-dum-dum-dum!"

sometimez,
my love.
i be
like
(B-lack)
"Niggaz! the insanity of it all!"

<u>Terminus.</u>

Knows NoThing.
Travels down the tree
Into another World
Of Work.
Metallurgy.

Dont wanna be a Wife.
Dont wanna be a Baby Mamma.
Any more.
No More.
No More.
No More.
No Moor.
No Muur.
No Mor.

Anymore.
Amore.
No amore
Any more.

Ishtar (Innana-O)

He say,

      "Maaayne, I just broke Easter!"

"My man!" (in my Denzel as Alonzo Harris voice)

"She Bible,

Esther too.

This Spring heat,

Esther and Estrum."

They are storytelling,

Our rituals.

Our celebrations,

The ram horns and holy sac-ram-ents,

The earthworms and beetles.

His seed in Her soil.

New beginnings,

Secret rituals to Mama Earth.

Pagan down to the symbols of eggs and sweet candy.

Easter, E/St(a)r.

(Spell/ing)

"EASTER"

TEAR	SEA
EAT	SEAT
STAR	TEAR
EAST	REST
TASER	SET
RAT	SAT

<u>288-S and Southmore</u>
Jes to let y'all know:
She lightening and thunder
Make a river where and flood when She please.

...

'Please be pleased with me-
Mines,
Ours.
'Round here
We been praying for change.'

...

"Warriors!"

"Papa Eshuooo-Elegbara! "(Ase!)"

Mama Oya!" "(Ase!)"

"Baba Shango!"

"(Ase!)"

"Mama Ochun!" "(Ase!)"

"Papa Oggun!"
"(Ase!)"

...

Today, We are remembering Our Warriors.

Memorial Day.

(veil)

...

She say,
The Devil is A Goddamn Lie.

...

"Very strange storm indeed."

Diaspora

Remember Algeria.
Art is Activism.
Its living with the vision.
Creating resistance pieces,
Love poems and poems about the times-
What Must Be Done.

Voodoo.
We need some voodoo too.
In this valley of dry bones.

Lucy

"in plain sight/
shine so bright/
Eye can't see/
infront of me."

<u>Sincerely, Leo</u>

Sunday. Praise God.

On yo off day.

Niggy sTardust.

First Betsy now Cecil.

Sun hard like gold.

Sweating and going on.

Y'all betta gon' on.

Sine, Shekinah.

P.S.

Harambé! Harambé. Harambé. Harambé. Harambé. Harambé. Harambé. Harambé. Harambé.

Prose. (Untitled)

"hello beautiful." she smiles coyly. he continues, "sweet heart, listen to my stories that i might woo you with my tales of adventure." she listens. she asks questions and he is encouraged to continue. she thinks, "this man is interesting and easy to talk too." he searches for his business card to give her. he will ask her to call... no he will ask for her phone number. she hears her name being announced to address the room. excusing herself she approaches the crowd. he thinks, "how cute. she sings or recites love poems." she looks at him, inhales and exhales slowly. closes her eyes and disappears...... she returns to applause and sweaty hands. she looks around and remembers where she is.. to steady her breath.. to smile and say, thank you. she feels open and exposed... 5, 4, 3, 2, 1... better. she is herself again... she smiles at him. he stares and says nothing 4, 3, 2, 1... he responds, "that was deep." his hand slips the card back into his pocket. he does not ask for her number... he sips his drink in silence, then excuses himself.. she doesn't watch him walk away.... she puts the ice cold water to her lips, and replenishes herself..... she knows. and is at peace with the unknown.

Submerge Within The Light

Now is the time for love poems.

Now

Is the time

For

Love

Poems.

Now

Is

The time

For love

Poems

Now is the time

For

Love poems

Now

Writing

Love poems

Time

For love.

Now

Is

The time.

S&M, A Series

(To Be Con't.)

Parts I & VI

S&M I

Shame

&

Mercy

S & M VI

Crucifying

The

Savior

<u>On July 19, upon reading a headline instigating a race riot during the Summer of (Not) Sweet '16.</u>

<u>Or, Colorable Laws.</u>

"when i was at the event and they took pictures and if you ain't know better you would think everybody came together but I didn't so don't group us together cause they on some other ish and I'm not cause I know Niggas are scared of revolution and jesus and the gold and silver cause you not looking cause "tada, a rabbit inside my hat" looking at the sun and can't cee so mabey I am like-minded in some ways just not the way of political prisoners like mumia and assata and sacrifices of their bodies just laying there and nobody moved. move not like move and bombs and terror and 911 and sadness no I'm silver and gold and coltan and this land is my land-this land is your land kumbaya singing cause the alternative is bloody like chicago."

Fill In The Black:

"Georgie Porgie

Pudding Pie.

Killed a boy then made his Mama

Cry.

Georgie

Must

(_ _ _)."

<u>Politics</u>

Authoritative and Submissive

Relationships

So many tricks

We keep getting dicked.

Free the Land.

#poinsettasandbabymamas
(Earth, AEarth)

Hoodoo 05082014

she sees what comes

she knows the order of things

her shells and beads and bones

made of earth and sound

she listens and watches

and strikes when the wind blows her back

on a Tuesday (Mars),

tuesdays

are

for

warriors.

we sharpen our blades, metals and mind on

tuesdays.

we hold ginger on the back of our tongue

binding spell are broken

on tuesdays.

uhuru.

uhuru.

uhuru sasa.

SKMT.

Tuff (Spoken Word)

"its tuff because the majority of imagery in media- television programs, commercials, and print- caters to european american demographics. while this gives other ethnicities the charge to create and promote their own programs (and competing for distribution), it also leaves our children to idolize images counter productive to their own developing self-esteem. this is what happens when nations of people are either forced to abandon/forget their culture, or choose to adopt another's culture as their own. the vehicles of positive senses of self such as mythologies, stories, legends, gods, and other psychological tools that provide a way to organize one's thoughts are no longer there to buffer against harms in the larger environment.... forward ever."

Red Wine and Green Olives

Red.
Red wine and green olives.
Black olives.
Feeling
Some type of way...
My current situation..
Is that what we say now??
Now..
Lord, please dont let me be misunderstood. ..
Or play the fool
Again.
I'll blame it on the Red
Red wine
Salty olives on my tongue
Feeling some type'a way....

NTR....
My badd,
Nature...

Prolly 'that' time of the month...

I mean, prolly 'that' time of the month...

U know..
When The Itch comes?
We still call it that, right?

The itch...

The insatiable urge to touch and tease and hunch and fuck...

Oh no....

Must be the red,
Red.
Red wine......
Red wine and olives.....
Bless your Sanctified eyes and ears...
Its those Spirits talkin...

"Lord, please dont let me be misunderstood. .."
Hallow Nina...
Wild is the Wind.
And
Me.
Unapologetically.
#Mycurrentsituation

Sweaty from honoring my womb and all She creates..
Created...
Will create...
Right?
"Love me, Love me, Love me... Say you do."
Or dont.
Either way...
Spell on you...
Like Palm Oil and Bible Papers...
Blame me...
I said it.
Did it...
Do it...

Well.
Thank You.
You.
Do.
Me.
This.
Way.

This.

Red.
Red wine.
And Green Olives....
Got me feeling some kinda way...
Must be ovulation...
Itchin' for a scratchin....

It comes and goes.

Naah,
Not really.

Sippin this Red.

Red wine.

Snuff

"how terrorism works.... she is me, easily. i already know what happened cause ive been there before. outspoken. she showed those devils her fangs and they tore her apart. to prove a point. just because. and for no reason other than, bow down black bitch. and i went a little crazy. and my sister had to heal me enuff, fill in the hole they keep diggin.... her reiki words... him. his innerG when i needed it... we need each other. cause this is how terrorism works, this is the silent part of war. the mind fuck. the chippin away at sanity, the weakening of immune and emotion and spirit... gunning for our souls. the soul-less ones. and every time i see them, i look through them. a little terrified cause my mouth is black like fuck you. eloquently articulate, like i know my rights pig.... i have the right to remain silent? i have the right to remain violent? my rites. my rites. my rites. love self, love family, love friends and a-alikes, love community, love the nation we build with each seed. love in spirals, deep

and all powerful black holes. black. no one escapes.
fuck terror. i know y, fear of a black universe."

925

"Cause we are embarrassed

Talking that Black

Don't wanna digg too deep

Feelings?

Feeling crazy.

B.u.t. sane enough to see.

925.

Won't make a sacrifice outta me.

Won't make a victim outta me.

Won't make a unavenged martyr outta me.

Won't tell my family, "Sorry."

Ain't sorry.

Ain't sorry.

Ain't sorry.

This old race.

This older war.

Amiri,

"Who civil?

Who lied?

Who civilized?

Who's civilized?

Who? Whoooooo?

Who gives them orders to shoot?"

925

Silver bullets pointed back at you.

(Werewolves- Rome)

<u>on a Thursday (Jupiter)</u>,

she knows-

money comes, money goes.

her hand stays open to give and receive,

learned how to say goodbye from the trees,

learned mercy and divine providence

on dark nights with full moons.

new moons are for silent, secret words

and buried deeds.

SouthWest eGypsTy

the metropolis/"novus ordo seclorum"/tricky, tricky/love me, need me/never leave me/implant trees/ass implants/stuck-up assholes/6 inch stilleto's/looking down on folks looking up/wanna be/free/in the city/municipalities/taxes and fines/churches and mosques/liquor stores and walmarts/my block tough/until/the water bill aint paid/S.H.I.T.

An Invitation

phases of my moon/dont be scared/i was born in summer/5 days after the new year/26/just like grandma/with watermelon seeds/and red dirt/friday fish frys/embracing the night sky/visible off roads/deep in east texas/country/im country/easy living/porch swings/simple things like cool breezes/reading tea leaves/and chicken bones/dont be scared/tobacco and gin/creek baptisms/talking shit under shade trees/full moons we gather/new moons we lay low/waxing and waning/we love/fight/dance/fuck/trade stories and pick peas from the garden/dont be scared/the city/swallows the stars/and sucks the luminescence out of Moon's children/i am not scared

unplugged, l.boogie now and forever

"So automatic/on autopilot/simulacra, far from original/non-intentional/un-individual/sheeple/kneeling before their stolen steeples/needing a messiah/ascending no higher/than them and they/whatever he say/see the games she play/taught from day one to follow/and obey/hold all questions and requests/the rest will be advised/once the verdict is read/here we go again/moor fathers shot dead/moor mothers murdered/the hypocrisy/them pretending to be/while sacrificing all who oppose/I suppose, this is kharma/reciprocity for not ending this//sooner//a natural progression/the constant devolution/same ole non-solutions/dress it up and maybe no one will recognize/pull the wool over your eyes/lies and bills/electric and water/lets have a truly honest conversation/i think we outta/what you was saying about slaughter/something bout buying fashion brands for your daughter/living in this fiction/your son fits the description/and will be profiled as such/lets see if he acts tuff/lets see if you're black enuff/or just chatter/your opinion doesn't matter/in the year of the beast/move ya dollars and move ya feet/never retreat."

civiliter mortuus
for eric garner

and renisha mcbride

and sandra bland

and tamir rice

and trayvon martin

and ray anthony peacock
and him, and him, and him, and him, and him, and him
and her, and her, and her, and her, and her, and her, and her
and him, and him, and her,
and the too many murdered while we stand and watch in terror...

dont judge us
too harshly
we dont remember
wasnt raised with truth
shown we were less than

unworthy of decency and grace
no mercy
not even from Jesus...

Black like the colour of sin.

July 2010

no need 2 front like tounge-on-body doesnt xcite me/his big on my little playing over in my thoughts/laughing and biting and wrestling his will/will get my panties in a punch/flesh on flesh-pleasure principal

fantasy seeker/carnal backstrokes and hydraulic pokes/strong, wett contractions/his satisfied reaction/we, fully human and flesh/yet, shhhhh...she deep.

AZ,

in the tradition of The Last Poets

"niggaz.

niggaz been doing the same shit

they been doing

cuz they dont

cee

no other way.

niggaz.

niggaz talk

and judge

and fuss

and feel

a way about

other niggaz

doing

different.

niggaz.

niggaz.

"i loooooove niggaz.

but one thing i do not love

about niggaz...."

Precious

"Foolish of me to think Blue Moon would pass without requiring my tithes. Me, daughter of Night.
Perhaps, had it not been for blood, gifted from earth and sea and She. Activating my inner-whispering Knowing.

He lured me out my cave with honey and sweet smells of ylang-ylang, then challenged me to fight. Confidently sang his warning, 'Only one of us will win and walk away'. Initially reluctant to fully engage him,

respectfully submitting to the Moon Daughter's tradition of reserving the majestic fullness for admirers and lovers. His strategic advances met with coy retreats. Until he aimed for my heart. Until he sought to decapitate my head.

Awakening Dragon.

As I rize to morning dew and soft croaking toadfrogs, I find myself wiser and more aware of

Her. With his blood on my hands. A dragonslayer's body at my feet.

A treasure released."

"let cho soul glo'"

"Raise a black fist to sho' nuff black power.

Black images.

Cleopatra Jones, The First.

Before Max Julien changed time and influenced the future.

And warner brothers abracadabra'd Cleo into a sex kitten. Before all the soul brothers wanted to trade their dishiki's in

4 pimp cups.

Glitches on de'javu."

Salty Water (My Uzi)

Word to Heavy D.

Hoe Magick dont work on me.

Neural Pathways (NIA)

"Its in your DNA child.

Its in your DNA.

Its part of who you are child,

It makes you who you are today.

Its running through your veins

Encoded in your blood.

It whispers from the grave,

It twinkles up above.

It's in your DNA child.

It's in your DNA."

Ammi_Android, 112016

shake down, shake dance, shekere, shimmy
he say, show me
she say, gimme gimme

shake down, shake dance, snake trance, shimmy
he say, give it back now
she say, I've got plenty

what you do for one
you gotta do for the other
if she helps you smile
if she helps you smile
gotta do for the other
if she makes you smile

"Slide some oil to me.." 05182014

love looks like,

lend me some light

smile at me and open my heart to the possibilities

challenge me to grow towards our source

be my mirror so i can see myself in you

my love, whom i adore

stay in my thoughts like,

pineapple upside-down cake

a sweet taste in my mouth

and when our love looks unkept and inconvenient

i wont paint it pretty again

i will stare love down until love speaks

from the other side.

Love, Prince Malcolm Shabazz

no romantic notions/no puritan messianic fantasy/he god/self made/searching for peace in amerikkka/salam in this wilderness/where power is stolen/and hope is given freely/like g.m.o. freebies/and programming on tv//real people so real shit/cookie cutter leaders need not apply/ brainwashing lies about diplomacy/he, accepted his legacy/brought solutions to the streets/coalitions and gangs/striving to change/building for the betterment/for the people/his labors of love/ atonement and restitution/there is no confusion/ only respect/tattooed tears"

truly, 17

About the Author:

Keshia "K. Boogie" Shantae is a multi-disciplinary artist currently residing in Houston, TX. She is a social anthropologist, professional educator, and initiated spiritualist. She uses her many talents and passions while crafting her poetic commentaries on the world as she sees it. As a spoken word artist, she travels the U.S., winning SLAM competitions and sharing her works with audiences large and small.

Her podcast can be heard Mondays, 9pm (CST): www.blogtalkpodcast.com/CircleSisters

To Contact, Email: templeofshe42@gmail.com.

Website: www.Zora42.com

"I need you."

Thank You!
Your support is appreciated.

www.ingramcontent.com/pod-product-compliance
Lightning Source LLC
Chambersburg PA
CBHW032054150426
43194CB00006B/525